KALPAVRIKSHAM

MY SOUL MAGNIFIES THE LORD

P. MARY VIDYA PORSELVI

My mother-in-law Masilla Mary

and My father-in-law Amalorpavam

who bear the names of Blessed Virgin Mary

and taught me the value of Rosary

Contents

Contents

Contents

Contents

Contents

Contents

Contents

Preface

My soul magnifies the Lord
My heart rejoices in Mother Earth
My mind delights in Her Praise

The book draws inspiration from the Magnificat, celebrating Mary's song of praise on one hand and acknowledging her as one of the esteemed daughters of Mother Earth on the other. It aims to praise Blessed Virgin Mary as an embodiment of universal motherhood, possessing qualities akin to Mother Earth. The term "*Kalpavriksham,*" meaning a "wish-fulfilling tree," symbolizes Mary's significance in connecting earthly existence with the divine realm, serving as a channel between humanity and her divine Son, as well as the almighty creator.

The name 'Mary' has been intertwined with my life since the day of my christening, stemming from a family tradition of devout reverence towards Our Lady. Immersed in Marian teachings since childhood, my education and subsequent exploration of feminism and ecofeminism only deepened my appreciation for Mary's spiritual essence and stirred me on a quest for life-affirming silences and absences. Contrary to conventional belief, feminist and ecofeminist ideologies reinforced my faith in Mary's multifaceted role as a woman of strength and resilience. Viewing Mary through this lens, I perceive her as an ecological figure embodying various roles—wife, relative, farmer, shepherdess, goddess and above all, a mother whose nurturing wisdom and leadership qualities shaped her divine Son into a universal gift to humanity.

Through an ecofeminist perspective, I revisit biblical narratives concerning Mary and her family, exploring the profound interconnection between her upbringing and the teachings and miracles of Jesus. Delving deep into Mary's apparitions worldwide, as well as the divine mysteries, I humbly seek to throw light upon the relevance of Mary's experiences in contemporary contexts. Employing a poetic-interpretive approach, I have resorted to the Haiku - Senryu form of 17 syllables in a 5-7-5 pattern to convey my Marian thoughts and emotions.

Kalpavriksham refers to a Banyan Tree. Ecologically categorized into nine chapters, the book unfolds Mary's journey through metaphors, signs, symbols and imagery related to the growth of a tree: "Seeds of Confidence," "Sapling Promise," "Roots Nurture," "Soil Sustenance," "Sunshine Support," "Water Ways," "Canopy Cover," "Flower Power," and "Fruits of Faith." Mary, portrayed as a tree, captures the essence of life's cyclical journey. Like a hidden banyan seed waiting to sprout, Mary embodies the potential for growth and renewal, rooted in unwavering faith in the divine plan. With her husband Joseph's support, she nurtures her Son Jesus, laying a strong foundation for his transformative mission. As Jesus matures as a teacher, preacher, storyteller, and a leader, Mary provides steadfast support, akin to nourishing soil and invigorating sunshine. Her vital role expands to encompass protection, sustenance, and the propagation of faith, akin to a flourishing fruit bearing tree and nurturing new believers.

Quintessentially, central to Mother Mary's piety is a profound sense of immanence, through which she reinvents a form of earth-based spirituality that offers solace, hope, and peace to believers. In honoring Mary as a symbol of universal motherhood and divine instrument, the book serves as a humble tribute to her enduring legacy and timeless significance in the hearts of believers worldwide.

P. Mary Vidya Porselvi

Seeds of Confidence

1. Maria's Heart

Her magnified heart
dignified seed-humble hearth
in mystified Earth

2. Magnificat

Mamma Maria's soul
magnified the Lord before
He became seed One

3. Word Power

*She knew true power
of words as He was seed Word
born out of God's word*

4. Simple Yes

Generations call
Her blessed for seed-simple
"Yes" she truly said

5. Flower's Envy

Tender soft petals
envied Her seeded heart in
complete surrender

6. Her Story

7. Shining Star

Star led them to star
twinkling across horizons
of stellar sown hope

8. Heavenly Message

*She received divine
message, perceived heavenly
seed, conceived Her Son*

9. Fond Family

Maria knew She
sowed Jesus in her womb which
Joseph held in heart

10. Full of Grace

11. True Transformation

Timorous seed-maid
transformed into a goddess
accepting God's plan

12. Caring Conviction

Like peace loving lamb
in green pastures She followed
Good Shepherd in womb

13. Bonding Matters

14. Homeless Mother

*When women saw dull,
homeless, mother's faint, cheerless
face they felt pity*

15. Nativity Song

Angels sang sweetest
lullaby for newborn babe's
worn weary Mother

16. Her Friends

Winter night dare not
touch infant as Her fauna
friends were all around

17. Lamb's Wonder

Gentle lamb that lay
beside warm manger wondered
She was a goddess

Sapling Promise

18. Sure Serendipity

Silent winter night
was green miracle to lamb
and His kind Mother

19. Baptismal Cues

Did two gardeners
know their sons would sprout into
Baptist and baptized!

20. Lily Love

Her husband knew She
was purer than white lily
he held in his hand

21. Gifting Givers

Gold, frankincense, myrrh
were scions to family
of givers galore

22. Untiring Giving

She nourished Him like

magnanimous Magi who

rode on tireless search

23. Pastoral Lullaby

Before sun rise She
sings lullaby to grass lambs
that rest in Her arms

24. Sacred Doves

*She offered doves in
temple - As Holy Spirit
they returned as tongues*

25. Warm Gratitude

Ann and Joachim, He
humbly thanked for giving Him
mamma nature

26. Complete Surrender

Mamma taught Him true
meaning of rooted faith in
complete surrender

27. Amma's Faith

*Amma knew for sure
that Her Sun could even turn
water into wine*

28. Enchanting Teller

*Story-telling was
His magic baton, a branch
from loving mother*

29. Temple Tale

Reprimanding them
reminded Him of Miriam's
childhood chidings

30. Palm Sunday

From Mary He learnt
to be humble when he heard
Hosanna leaf hymns

31. Caring Multitude

He knew their hunger
and served them with love, first food
lesson from Mamma

32. Reminiscing Reverence

*Maria taught her Son
to respect women and He
remembered like roots*

33. Mary the Follower

Did Mary ever
meet Mary Magdalene to
share fangirl moments?

34. Women Knew

Woman in mass surge
decreed, blessed is His mother
who birthed and nursed Him

Roots Nurture

35. Discipleship Matters

36. Filial Piety

With devotion She
ingrained lamp of God
in Her folded hands

37. Lamp on a Stand

As a child, He saw
Her putting lamp on tall stand
to let the light shine

38. Good Soil

*When She sowed seeds on
good soil He knew it would grow
undisturbed by thorns*

39. Mustard Seed

Amidst cooking spree
She taught Him true value of
tiny mustard seed

40. Leaven Heaven

Kneading white flour with
His tender fingers He learnt
leaven is heaven

41. Treasuring Treasure

42. Utmost Preparation

Before setting out
to work Her Son was prepared
like grounded bridesmaids

43. Talent Trust

*Though She was given
one talent She used it to
form the Chosen One*

44. In Times of Need

Even as a child
He had seen His mamma as
a Good Samaritan

45. The Lost Coin

Playing around His
mother He found shiny lost
coin and Her joy

46. Proud Moment

Her heart filled with pride
when He sat on the mount like
Boss amidst huge mass

47. Labor of Love

48. Mary and Elizabeth

49. Like a Child

*Born to innocent
young mother, He always knew
worth of child-like heart*

50. Language of Love

His language was love
acquired from mother's
day of conception

51. Calm In Calm Out

He could even calm
storms outside, thanks to Mamma
He was calm within

Soil Sustenance

52. Sad Fig

For once mamma was
upset with Him for cursing
the fruitless fig tree

53. Fine Gentleman

When they tried to stone,
He stopped them as gentleman
born to fine lady

54. Prayer Task

*When He set out on
His mission, She prayed for Him
every fine minute*

55. Listening and Telling

56. Words of Solace

57. Maternal Agony

When they crowned Him with
thorns, She felt like a fish thrown
in hot boiling sand

58. Motherly Ecstasy

59. Knowing the Hungry

60. Pure Submission

Immaculate is
She who considered herself
as chosen vessel

61. Love Nest

Like Father bird he
prepared a warm nest where She
laid newborn fledgling

62. Donkey Said

With Her Son in womb
She was gentlest soul riding
on me like feather

63. Painful Path

He carried hard cross
uphill, making way through flood
of women's tears

64. Enduring Olives

Olive trees taught Her
to be stoic, in garden
of Gethsemane

65. She Prayed

She always had oil
in Her lamps and prayer in
Her contented heart

66. Mother Medium

As mediator,
Mamma shone like sun's rays soaking
dark green olive leaves

67. Meekness Forever

When He washed the feet
of disciples they recalled
Her meek upbringing

68. Curing the Needy

When He scorched sickness
they glorified His mother
for Her radiant Son

Sunshine Support

69. Living Spring

For Santa Maria
madre de dios deserves thanks
for breathing waters

70. She Permits

Sacrosanct passport
to reach the destination
of His divine nation

71. Calm Composer

She composed serene
musical piece of splendor
and deliverance

72. Morning Glory

Our Lady's mantle
blooms in hues of skies and seas
each lovely morning

73. Their stories

*Visitation to
Elizabeth's house confirmed
maternal magic*

74. Nature-vity

*Nature took care of
Her and family as a
sign of gratitude*

75. Profound Presentation

When Son was offered
She heard the divine calling
Her heart skipped a beat

76. Deep Discussion

Her heart overwhelmed
with pride when She saw Her Son
as thinking human

77. Supper with Love

She served first supper
and He served last supper with
love on silent nights

78. Tired Garden

Plants in the garden
forgot to breathe for awhile
seeing Her Son's angst

79. Pillar in Pain

Pillar felt the pain
when Her Son was whipped and scourged
for no fault of His

80. Thorns and Tears

His crown of thorns brought
tears of blood in Her eyes
on Calvary path

81. Timber Apology

Tree that gave wood to
make the cross apologized
to His sad Mother

82. Dead Dread

Her Son died, darkness
encapsulated the world
for a while in dread

83. Rising from Ashes

Her phoenix Son rose
from ashes of human sins
to replenish grace

84. Arc Crescendo

Ascending into
heaven He prepared a place
for loving Mother

85. Charismagic

Her Son offered His
body-blood as Eucharist
like every mother

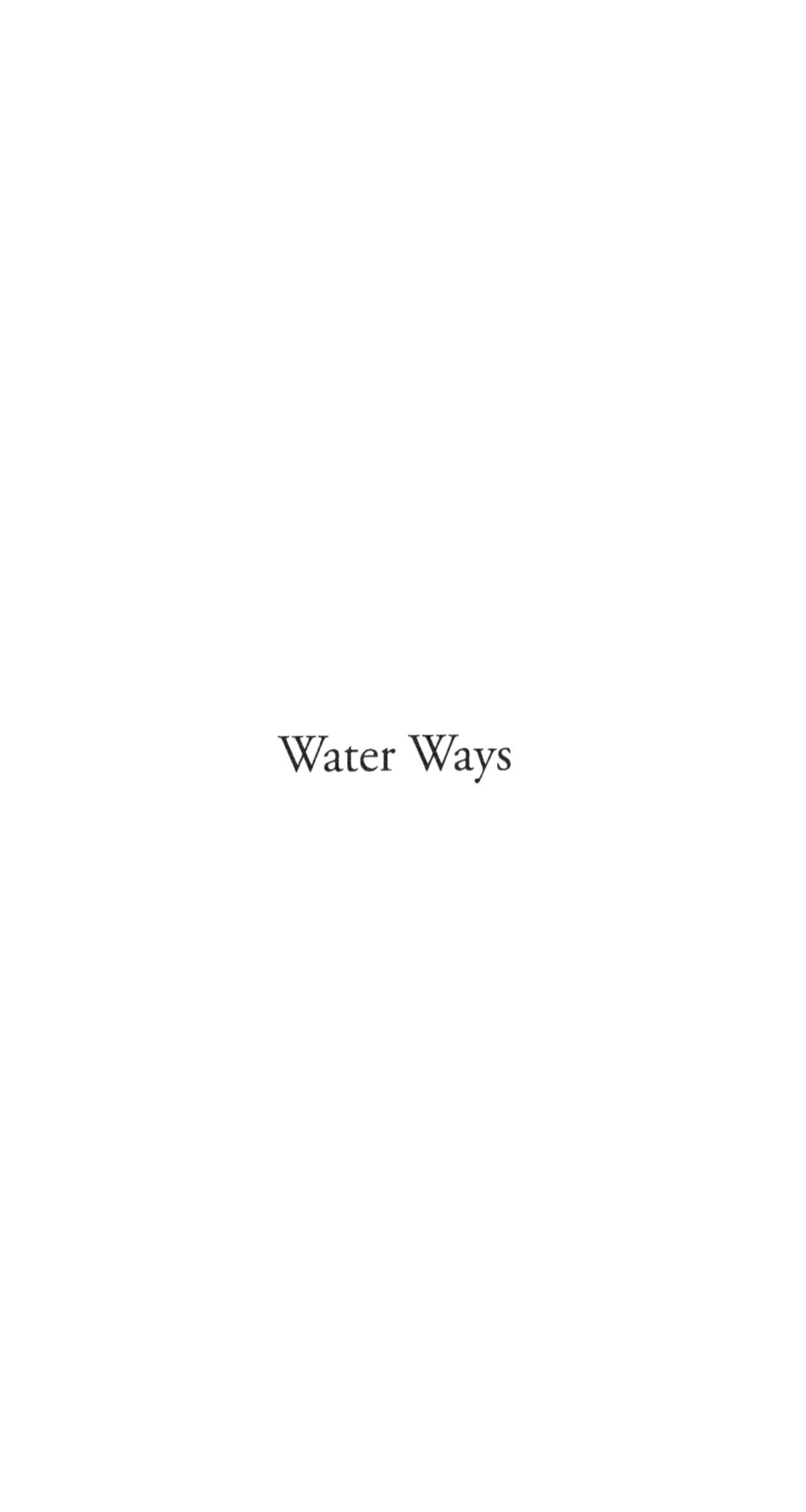

Water Ways

86. Daring Rise

Through transfiguration
Her Son emerged heroic
height for social good

87. Simple Supremacy

*She found power in
gentleness, meaning in truth,
sense in harmony*

88. Family Faith

She raised family
with care which planted faith
in dear Son's heart

89. Fledged Visitors

*Little doves feathered
outside Her home and She fed
them with great love*

90. Love is Respect

He knew that true love
meant respect because of His
Mother and Father

91. Silence is Strength

He learnt silence meant
strength from caring Mother and
carpenter Father

92. Risen Lamb

She did see Him rise
from dead as pristine lamb She
once held in Her arms

93. Kind Veronica

When she wiped His face
Mamma appreciated
her with a blessing

94. Demanding Peace

*Peace and calm that stopped
the storm was in His genes as
His tranquil Mother*

95. Living Soul

Those who utter Her
holy name finds their sincere
souls in endless bliss

96. Predestination

Bonding with Her word
day in - day out we reserve
a confirmed ticket

97. Green Pastures

Great great Granddaughter
of Aaron bore Good Shepherd
as per Divine Will

98. River Tree

*Like a lush green tree
by river She held head high,
still rooted to ground*

99. First Miracle

100. Real Cure

Every time He cured
a woman His Mamma's soul
magnified Her Lord

101. Father's Will

He looked up to His
Father and said "your will be
done" just like Mamma

102. Her Vision

Like a spectrum in
early morning dew She saw
His seeds of greatness

Canopy Cover

103. His Anger

*She admired anger
of Her Son in moments of
social injustice*

104. His Courage

*Dumbfounded by His
courage Mamma resolved to
take untrodden path*

105. His Truth

Lily flowers had
faith in true word of Her Lord
and remained in peace

106. His Name

Sparrows believed in
His plan and cherished Her day
without fear and doubt

107. Potent Fasting

She learnt how to fast
in Her younger days but He
taught an intense one

108. Teaching Walking

*She skilled Him to walk
on the land and was thrilled
when He walked on water*

109. Real Reclamation

110. Flood Feasting

111. Divine Doctor

112. Soul Helper

*Mary and Joseph
helped some. Their Son helped many
to align their souls*

113. Every Word

Because She conceived
Him as Divine Word every word
He said was divine

114. Her Visage

Woman who was cured
of her infirmities saw
Mother's grace in Him

115. Commanding Love

116. Water Wisdom

Looking at surface
color of seas Her son found
abundance within

117. Tree Truths

She taught Him to pray
observing skies like trees that
stay rooted below

118. Land Legend

He made His Mother
proud by telling fair legend
that last shall be first

119. Soil Sense

*Seeds that fell on good
soil helped seeds that fell among
rocks and thorny scrubs*

Flower Power

120. Plant Poetics

Unconditional love
and hope were like plant breathings
She taught Him early

121. Wings Wisdom

Birds of the skies flew
with mindfulness, She whispered
that He will provide

122. Fauna Notes

Lambs and calves around
newborn babe comforted Her
drained body and mind

123. Holy Acceptance

Genuflecting in
front of the Holy Spirit
She accepted His Word

124. Hallowed Spirit

Gifts, fruits, fire of
Holy Spirit she was endowed
for being honest

125. True Devotion

126. Tree Solution

With tenacity
of a tree by the living waters
She reigned sacred roost

127. Real Redemption

Rivers that carried
sins for ages recovered
grace in Marian seas

128. Astral Coronation

Moon and Stars raced to
crown our humble Lady as
sparkling diamonds

129. Mothering the Lord

For once, little milk
Selling lad mothered hungry
child of health goddess

130. Tempest Trust

Storms retreated in
fear when sailors recalled
Her Son's words 'Believe'

131. Star of the Sea

132. Care-Giver

Beschi paints Egypt-
-fleeing Mary a caring
human at Gaza

133. Kindling Renewal

134. Juan's Dream

Tepeyac valley
was filled with lightning rays
with our Lady's dream

135. Cloud Counsel

She chose to reside
in silver-lined rain clouds to
mentor missing sheep

136. She Sky Sees

Her eyes look up to skies
in gratitude- look down to
earth in servitude

Fruits of Faith

137. Eternal Spring

Gathering firewood
in countryside Bernadette
found spring of life

138. Mother of Healer

Mother of healer
touched the butter milk-selling
lame boy and cured him

139. Beads Shield

Fifty-three beads of
rosary serve as armor
to Her followers

140. Rare Refuge

Like waves of the sea
people throng to Her abode
with hope for refuge

141. Tender Rock

Gracing in Grotto
She stands tall in faithful hearts
like dense solid rock

142. Solid Sobriety

Queen of sobriety
rules the masses with scepter
of grace and calm

143. Shepherd Children

Little lamb-like kids
She chose to reveal secrets
of perpetual hope

144. Full Circle

She was full circle -
creator - nurturer with
crown of gentleness

145. Bead Design

When prayer beads are
coupled with conscientious deeds
signs of grace appear

146. Pure Protection

Fortification
is sure blessing for those who
praise Her lovely name

147. Rosary Rings

In a world filled with
distractions, the sacred loop
is a safety valve

148. Rescue Time

Children at wartime
wonder when will Mother and
Her Son rescue them

149. Healing Duo

Mother and Son are
healers of body, mind, soul
in times of dire need

150. Aurora Glows

hues of blue and pink
radiance engulfs skies with
Her serene spirits

151. Servant Sovereign

152. Mother Earth

153. Heart-Hearth-Home

She was at home in
Her heart. Her soul was at Her
home. Earth became Home